Cat Out of the Bag

IRENE YATES

Illustrated by Amanda Wood

PACIFIC
LEARNING

© 2001 Pacific Learning
© 1999 Written by **Irene Yates**
Illustrated by **Amanda Wood**
US Edit by **Rebecca Weber McEwen**

This Americanized Edition of *Cat Out of the Bag,* originally
published in English in 1999, is published by arrangement
with Oxford University Press.

05 04 03 02 01
10 9 8 7 6 5 4 3 2 1

Published by
  Pacific Learning
  P.O. Box 2723
  Huntington Beach, CA 92647-0723
  www.pacificlearning.com

ISBN: 1-59055-046-3
PL-7411

Contents

1
Surprise!

Kirandip noticed the cat sleeping in Mrs. Weston's kitchen window.

"You'll never guess what I saw!" she said to her mom.

"What's that?" Mom asked.

"Mrs. Weston has a cat!"

Mom shook her head. "I doubt it."

Kirandip said, "I just saw it…"

"How can Mrs. Weston have a cat?" Mom said. "She never said anything to me about it."

That was true, and they talked all the time. Whenever Mom was out running errands, she did Mrs. Weston's shopping too. Kirandip would deliver the food or supplies every day after school.

Kirandip never minded doing this. She had nothing else to do after school, because she hadn't made any friends yet. She'd had friends at her old school in Chicago. She had known them forever. She was at home there.

Then Dad had to move to Baltimore for his job – and Mom and Kirandip had come early, to find a place to live and get Kirandip started at her new school.

Now after nearly a whole month, Kirandip hadn't found a single friend.

Mom was always saying, "Give people a chance, Kirandip. You just have to find something to break the ice…"

Mom's voice broke into her thoughts. "Come on, Kirandip! Forget the cat – you don't want to be late for school!"

All the same, Kirandip was sure she *had* seen a cat… hadn't she?

2
Impossible

All day long Kirandip thought about the cat. She was *sure* she had seen it. It was orangey-brown, fluffy, fat, and had a contented face. It had been asleep in the sunny window.

She made up her mind to ask Mrs. Weston about it.

"Hi, it's only me!" Kirandip shouted, letting herself into Mrs. Weston's front gate that afternoon. She banged the gate hard.

Mrs. Weston was almost deaf. This is why Kirandip made lots of noise. She didn't want to take her by surprise and scare her when she walked in.

The old lady called out to her from the kitchen. She was always happy when Kirandip came over after school.

"Hello! Hello, my dear! It's time we had a snack!"

Kirandip happily made a pot of mint tea. It was a tradition they followed every afternoon. When Mom was at work, Kirandip always stayed at Mrs. Weston's house.

There was no sign of a cat anywhere. However, there was a saucer of milk on the kitchen floor, next to the stove.

Kirandip caught her breath. She carried the tray to Mrs. Weston in the family room.

"Let's have some cookies too," Mrs. Weston said – this was her part of their tradition. She jumped up from her chair and sped over to the cupboard.

Kirandip smiled to herself. Even though Mrs. Weston was almost ninety years old, she was very independent. If Kirandip tried to help, it would just hurt Mrs. Weston's feelings.

Kirandip poured each of them a mug of tea.

The old lady offered her the cookies.
"Today I think we deserve two!"

Kirandip took a chocolate chip and a
pecan crunch. Mrs. Weston grabbed two
huge cinnamon snickerdoodles.

"So, Kirandip, tell me what you did at school today," she said merrily.

"Not much," Kirandip said. She happily munched on the cookies – her favorites. "We had art this afternoon."

Then she had an idea. "We painted pictures of cats," she said.

Mrs. Weston seemed to jump. She took a long gulp of her tea and paused before she said, "That's nice. I used to like painting when I was a girl."

Then she changed the subject. "Did you have P.E.?"

"I painted a black cat," Kirandip said. She watched the old woman carefully. "I painted a tortoiseshell cat too."

The old woman's eyes never left her mug of tea. There was a long silence.

"Then," Kirandip said, "I painted an orange cat." She paused.

The air seemed to hold its breath. "It looked like the one that was asleep in your kitchen window this morning."

The old lady stiffened. She stared at Kirandip.

"What cat?" she said. Somehow her shaky voice seemed to be coming from far away.

Kirandip proceeded carefully. "There was a cat in your kitchen this morning. In the window," she said. Then she added, "It was stretched out, fast asleep."

"Oh, no," Mrs. Weston said, shaking her head. "You made a mistake. There's no cat here!" She laughed – a little nervously, Kirandip thought.

Kirandip frowned. She *had* seen the cat. She knew it, but she wasn't about to accuse her old friend of telling lies. Mrs. Weston was too good to her.

"Well," she said at last, "I thought I did. If you say I didn't, though..." She paused.

Mrs. Weston clicked her teeth. "I don't see how you could have," she said. She picked up her mug. "Could you pour me another cup of tea? Then you can tell me what you did in P.E."

She's hiding something, Kirandip thought. *I didn't say we had P.E. today. She's trying to change the subject again.*

Kirandip put the teapot and the mugs on the tray and walked toward the little kitchen. That was when she heard the noise. *Meow.*

It seemed to be coming from behind
the door to the living room. *Meow!*
There it was again!

Kirandip glanced quickly at Mrs. Weston. The old lady hadn't heard the noise at all. She was smiling at Kirandip and pointing into the kitchen.

"Make us some hot chocolate if you'd prefer, dear."

Then it came again. *Meow!*

Suddenly Mrs. Weston seemed to guess why Kirandip was standing still.

"What is it?" she said anxiously. "What's the matter?"

"I hear something," Kirandip said. "It's coming from the living room. I think it's a cat... crying!"

All the color drained out of Mrs. Weston's face.

"You can hear it?" she said nervously.

Kirandip nodded.

Mrs. Weston stared down at her hands. "Oh dear," she said pitifully. "Now everybody will find out. I'm going to get into terrible trouble. Now they'll be able to get rid of me!"

Kirandip stared at Mrs. Weston, horrified. What did she mean – *get rid of her*?

The old lady began to cry. "You're not supposed to have pets here! It's not my fault! The cat just came! I couldn't turn it away – it likes me! If the landlord finds out, I'll be done for!"

"They can't get rid of you just because you have a cat!" Kirandip said, upset.

"Can't they!" she said angrily. "They want me out of here so they can raise the rent and get new tenants!"

Her face was red; her eyes smoldered with furious fire. "That's what they've been trying to do for ages!"

Kirandip's mouth opened and stayed open. Mrs. Weston couldn't be right. She just couldn't.

"Anyway," the old lady continued, "it's even worse than that! You don't know the half of it!"

Kirandip was puzzled. "What?"

Suddenly, the old lady collapsed back into her chair. "I don't know what I'm going to do," she sobbed. "The cat's going to have kittens."

3

Sworn to Secrecy

The cat was a beautiful tortoiseshell.

"Tortoiseshells are always queens,"
Mrs. Weston told Kirandip. She stroked
the cat gently as it curled up on her lap.

"I've known striped orange cats, and
they always have bold personalities.
These patchwork ones have always been
my favorites, though."

"She's wonderful," Kirandip said. "I
bet her kittens will be wonderful too. So
what's her name?"

"I don't know what her real name is. I just call her Kitty," Mrs. Weston said.

Kirandip bit her lip. She could see how her friend already loved the cat.

"What do you feed her?"

Tight-lipped, the old lady said, "She shares my dinner. I can't ask your mom to get me any cat food, because then she'd know. I really don't mind," she said bravely.

Mrs. Weston continued, "Kitty will just eat what I eat. She's very hungry, but that's because of her babies."

"When will they be born?"

Mrs. Weston shook her head. "I'm not sure," she said, "but it won't be long now. Listen, you *are* my friend, aren't you? The cat has to be our secret. Please don't tell anybody, all right?" Her eyes misted over. "If you do…"

Kirandip was saved from answering by the sound of the back gate. "I think it's Mom!" she said, relieved.

"Quick!" Mrs. Weston hissed. "Put Kitty in the living room!"

Kirandip grabbed the cat and raced for the door into the front room.

The cat gave a little grunt of protest as it was pushed into the other room. Kirandip's heart missed a beat. *Please don't let Mom hear her!*

"Helloooo!" Mom called out as she came in through the kitchen.

"Hello, Surinder," Mrs. Weston sang in an unruffled way. She was acting as though nothing was going on.

Mom looked at them both.

"Is everything all right?" she asked.

They both nodded, avoiding each other's eyes. Mom gave them a long, cool glance. "Good," she said at last.

Kirandip was *sure* she suspected something.

There was an awkward silence and then Mom said, "Let's go, Kirandip. I'm making samosas. You can help and then bring some to Mrs. Weston later. Come and get changed out of your school clothes…"

Just as she was leaving, Kirandip had an idea. "I have to go down to the convenience store for Mrs. Weston," she said casually.

For a moment, Mom looked very surprised. Kirandip had always been too timid to go before. "What...?" she began. She paused and then said, "Okay, but hurry up – it will be dark soon." Then off she went.

Mrs. Weston said, "I didn't ask you to pick up anything for me!"

"I know you didn't," Kirandip said. "I just thought it would be a good idea to go and get some regular cat food for Kitty. It's better for her."

For some reason, she wasn't the least bit scared.

4
Rules Are Rules

Kirandip couldn't really believe that someone could be thrown out of their house just for keeping a cat.

She wished she had someone to talk to at school, but who? It wasn't exactly the sort of thing she could start asking in class. They'd think she was weird.

She decided she would ask her dad when he came to visit during the weekend.

That Friday evening, as soon as he sat down, Kirandip went to talk to him.

"Dad, can we have a pet?"

Mr. Singh looked over the top of the newspaper he was reading.

"A pet, Kiri? What do you mean, a pet? You're at school all day, your mom is at work in the hospital, and I am constantly traveling back and forth."

He laughed a kind laugh. "No. It's not a good idea to have a pet. Who would look after it?"

"Well, could we have one if we wanted one? A dog? A cat?"

Mr. Singh put down his paper. "Kiri, that would be difficult. I don't think we can have animals in this house."

"Why not?"

He shrugged. "Because the landlord says so. Maybe he doesn't like them. Maybe he's worried about fleas and things. I don't know."

"What would happen if we got one and we didn't tell him?"

Mr. Singh grinned at her. "I think we would probably have to look for a new house!" he said. Then he chuckled to himself and started reading his newspaper again.

So it was true. Kirandip swallowed hard. She didn't know what to do. She couldn't possibly tell her mom or dad the secret.

She also knew that Mrs. Weston wouldn't get rid of the cat, especially with the kittens due. Her secret was bound to be discovered one day.

Before anyone found out, however,
there was suddenly a lot more than one
cat to worry about.

5
The Birth Day

On Wednesday afternoon, Mrs. Weston was waiting anxiously by her gate when Kirandip came over after school.

"Quick! Quick!" she whispered. "Oh, my goodness! What a terrible day I've had!" She grabbed Kirandip's arm and began to pull her toward the house.

Kirandip's heart skipped. What had happened?

"The kittens!" Mrs. Weston said. "She had the kittens!" She bulldozed Kirandip into the living room.

Kirandip had never been in there before. Her eyes widened. The room looked just like a picture she'd seen in a history book at school – it was all brown and gloomy.

There was a huge old armchair next to the window.

"That's my husband Bill's chair," Mrs. Weston said when she saw Kirandip looking at it. "He always used to sit there and watch the world go by."

The room had a damp, musty smell; not like the living room in Kirandip's house, which was bright and pretty and smelled of potpourri.

Kirandip couldn't see Kitty anywhere.

"Look!" Mrs. Weston said excitedly. She pointed to a glass cabinet full of old cups and plates.

Kirandip looked again.

Kitty was there all right, curled up underneath it.

It looked as though she had squeezed in and made a little nest. She was in a cardboard box that was squashed underneath the cabinet.

The cat gave Kirandip a startled look, as if to say, "Don't you dare come near me or my kittens!"

Kirandip stretched out her hand. She bent down and made a little mewing noise. "It's all right, Kitty," she murmured. "I'm not going to hurt you."

The cat just stared at her.

Then Kirandip saw something move.
A tiny kitten poked its head out from
underneath its mother's body. It gave a
little cry.

The kitten looked as if it didn't have any fur, and its eyes were tightly closed.

"Oh!" Kirandip gasped.

Mrs. Weston's voice boomed in Kirandip's ear. "She had seven of those little cuties! Seven kittens!"

Seven! *Oh no*, Kirandip thought. That would let the cat out of the bag for sure! How would they keep them secret? One cat they could manage, but eight...?

Impossible!

6

More Trouble!

"I'm sure Kiri and our neighbor are up to something!" Kirandip heard her mom say to her dad over the telephone. "She's over there all the time. I have to keep calling her to come home. Even stranger, she keeps volunteering to go to the convenience store..."

Kirandip sat on the stairs to listen.

"I have no idea what they're up to," Mom said. "I'll tell you one thing, though. You really need to get to the bottom of it when you get home on Friday – because I can't!"

Oh no! Kirandip crept back upstairs to her bedroom.

She knew that if her dad started to ask her what was going on, in the end she would give in and tell him. He had that kind of a way with her.

She could be vague with her mom and make all kinds of excuses. She wouldn't exactly lie to her... but she couldn't do that with her dad. He always seemed able to get to the truth.

"I don't know what we're going to do!" Kirandip told Mrs. Weston.

The kittens – two orange ones, three tortoiseshells, and two gray-and-brown striped ones – were getting bigger.

To tell the truth, they were beginning to be kind of a nuisance.

They were almost five weeks old now.

Kitty was worn out. The little ones kept racing after her, jumping up to drink milk. They clung on to her no matter how hard she tried to shake them off.

Mrs. Weston and Kirandip had tried to get them to lap milk or eat food from a saucer, but they wouldn't touch it.

Kirandip had bought a litter box and bags of litter from the convenience store. She had tried to keep her mom from seeing her, but even that had turned out to be a mistake.

For starters, training the kittens wasn't easy; they had accidents everywhere. The litter box had to stay in the living room so that Mom wouldn't see it, so the room smelled horrible.

Also, because the box was too heavy for Mrs. Weston, Kirandip had to keep emptying it in the outside can. Gross!

Then, every afternoon, when Mom came to pick her up, Mrs. Weston had to find an excuse to rush them both out of the house. She didn't want Kirandip's mom to have time to smell anything, or hear the kittens chasing around the living room.

Kirandip knew they couldn't go on like that forever. Maybe she would have to tell her dad on Friday when he came home, after all.

But what if she did, and he told the landlord? What if the landlord came over and made Mrs. Weston leave?

If he did, where would poor Mrs. Weston go?

7
Disaster!

Kirandip worried about the problem
that whole week.

She hadn't minded talking to people
since she'd started running errands
for Mrs. Weston. Now she wondered
whether she should ask in class if
anybody wanted a kitten.

She began to tell Sophie, a girl in her
class, but then she decided against it.
What if they all came knocking on the
door, asking to see the kittens? How
would she explain *that* to Mom?

On Friday afternoon, she rushed to
Mrs. Weston's as usual. When she got
there, there was no excited welcome,
which surprised Kirandip.

"It's just me!" Kirandip shouted as she
let herself in.

Nothing. No sound. *Where was Mrs.
Weston?*

Then Kirandip heard something that
made her heart stop. It was a low
moaning sound, and it was coming
from the living room.

Kirandip rushed through the open door, stepping over mewling kittens on her way.

Kitty looked up at her with weary eyes, from high up on the back of Mrs. Weston's husband's chair.

She seemed to say, "I've had just about enough of this. Look what they've done now!"

Then Kirandip saw Mrs. Weston.

Her friend was lying in a heap in front
of the fireplace. She was all tangled
up with the brass fire irons, and the
cardboard box from under the cabinet.

What a mess! Even the litter box was
spilled all around her.

"Kirandip, I tripped over one of the
kittens," Mrs. Weston gasped. "I
bumped my head..." Then she took a
deep breath and her eyes closed in her
pale face.

Kirandip's stomach did somersaults. *Was Mrs. Weston seriously hurt? What was she supposed to do?*

Around her, the kittens leaped and scampered and scurried, catching each other's tails in their teeth.

They looked as if there was nothing else to do in the world but play.

Kirandip remembered fainting once. She'd been out shopping with her mom. She'd felt really hot and shaky and then, suddenly, she fainted.

All she remembered about it was water being splashed on her face and then coming to in the store manager's office.

Maybe Mrs. Weston had just fainted.

Quickly, she rushed into the kitchen and found a bowl. She filled it with water, and grabbed the dish towel from the countertop.

Then she raced back into the living room, trying not to step on any of the kittens as she went.

They were still jumping around as though there was nothing wrong.

Kirandip knelt down beside her friend. "Mrs. Weston?" she whispered.

She could feel her heart thumping as she soaked the dish towel in the water, squeezed it out, and smoothed it over Mrs. Weston's face. "Please be okay!"

Suddenly, Mrs. Weston stirred. She gave a little sigh and licked her lips.

Kirandip folded the damp towel and gently laid it on Mrs. Weston's forehead. The old woman's eyes flickered open.

"Stay there!" Kirandip said – thinking it was an odd thing to say even as she said it. She removed the towel and ran to get a cup of water.

She put her arm under Mrs. Weston's head and lifted it. Then she held the cup of water to Mrs. Weston's mouth.

In a few minutes, Mrs. Weston was feeling much better. The color came back into her cheeks.

Kirandip grabbed the cushions from under Kitty. Then she struggled to prop up Mrs. Weston and tuck the cushions under her. She added a few more from another chair to make sure her friend was comfortable.

"What happened?" Kirandip asked.

Mrs. Weston gave a huge sigh. "I thought I'd get Kitty away from the kittens for a rest. When I came in, they were right under my feet. I tried to shoo them away..." Mrs. Weston paused.

"Well, somehow I managed to trip over one of the little rascals. When I was trying to catch myself, my foot caught on the litter box – whoosh! Flat on my back I went, and then I couldn't get back up."

"Well, you probably shouldn't try to," Kirandip said seriously. "You might have broken something. We'll just have to wait here until Mom comes." She looked at her friend anxiously. "Maybe I should call an ambulance…"

"Don't!" Mrs. Weston said, alarmed. "I'm not going anywhere in any ambulance. Please just do something about the cats before your mom gets here. Oh, I know. Take them upstairs and shut them in the bedroom."

Kirandip stared at her. Didn't Mrs. Weston understand? It was all over. She couldn't keep the cats a secret any longer. "But..." Kirandip started to say.

"No buts about it, Kirandip," Mrs. Weston said, her voice suddenly harsh. "You have to hide the cats. Otherwise people will find out, and then..." She lowered her voice and spoke in the most woeful tone Kirandip had ever heard, "they'll make me leave my home."

8
Taking Charge

Kirandip sat on the floor, thinking about how she could move the kittens. She'd have to grab two of them at a time. She'd have to take those two up the stairs and shut them in a room.

Then she'd have to come back down and get some more. How on earth would she keep the first two from escaping while she was getting the second two? They were so fast, and so full of energy...

Then there was Kitty herself. It didn't seem right to move her. She was so comfortable on the back of that old armchair.

Besides, she wouldn't take kindly to Kirandip picking her up.

Come to think of it, she wouldn't be very happy about Kirandip taking the kittens away from her.

What if Kitty thought she was trying to steal them? What if Kitty tried to stop her in some way?

It was not going to be easy.

"You'd better hurry up, dear," Mrs. Weston said, "because your mom will be here any minute. What if she finds us in this pickle? What are we going to do?"

"What are we going to say to her," Kirandip wailed, "when she asks us what happened?"

Mrs. Weston looked at Kirandip blankly. "I guess we'll just have to say I tripped," she suggested.

"Yes," Kirandip said, "but what about..." She waved her arm at the cat litter everywhere. "What about all the rest of this?"

It was going to be impossible to clean it up before her mom got there, and Kirandip knew it.

Then another thought struck her.

She could almost hear her mom say, "Maybe Mrs. Weston shouldn't live on her own anymore."

It may be true, Kirandip realized. Anyway, how could Mrs. Weston stay here with eight cats? Kirandip couldn't keep coming over and cleaning up after them – at least not for eight of them.

What will she do when they start growing up?

What if the kittens start having babies too?

What if all the female kittens had kittens of their own, and then those kittens had kittens, and then… It was pretty clear it would be a disaster.

Before you could turn around, there would be hundreds of cats in the house. Even Mrs. Weston couldn't cope with that, no matter how independent she wanted to be!

Suddenly, Kirandip knew what she had to do.

"Okay," she said, taking charge. "I'm going to make you a cup of tea. Then I'll do what I can to clean this place up. Then," she said, her mind made up, "we'll wait for Mom and we're going to tell her *exactly* what happened!"

Mrs. Weston's face crumpled. "I thought you were my friend," she said sulkily, "but you're not. You just want to get rid of me too."

55

9

Discovered

Mom couldn't have looked more
confused when she walked into the
kitchen and had to step over the frisky
kittens. "What's going on in here?"

Breathlessly, Kirandip began to explain.

"There was this cat, and Mrs. Weston
said the landlord would make her move
if he found out. Then the kittens came.
Then we had to get a litter box. Then
she tripped. And then..."

Mom's face turned pale. "Who fell? Who?" she demanded. Before Kirandip could answer she had rushed into the living room.

There was Mrs. Weston, still in a heap on the floor, dabbing away at the tears that rolled down her cheeks.

"You're going to be just fine," Mom said. "Let's see if anything's broken."

Briskly, she checked Mrs. Weston for broken bones. When she was sure nothing was seriously wrong, she helped her to her feet and sat her in Bill's chair.

"Kirandip, you did a good job," she said. "I'm glad you kept Mrs. Weston where she was – you handled it perfectly. I'm sure nothing is broken. It's probably shock more than anything. Now then, about these cats…"

Mrs. Weston began to weep again.

"She thinks the landlord will throw her out of the house," Kirandip explained, "because of the cats."

"We won't let that happen," Mom said firmly. "Your father will take care of it when he gets home."

Kirandip drew in her breath. "Do you think so? Really?"

"Of course," her mother replied. "There is nothing my Ranjit cannot do. Now, let's get the rest of this picked up, shall we?"

10

The Next Step

It was true. Dad had not been home long before he began to straighten out everything. First, he called the landlord.

"We've changed the rules a little – I don't mind tenants having one cat!" the landlord laughed. "One cat isn't bad!"

Then he said to Dad, "If the house is getting to be too much for Mrs. Weston, there's a vacant apartment she could have. It's just down by the convenience store – there aren't even any stairs. Then I could rent that house to a family."

They all went to visit Mrs. Weston. Dad told her what the landlord had said. "So," he explained, "you'd be much more comfortable. There's a lady on the top floor who could keep an eye on you, and we could help you move in!"

Mrs. Weston's eyes flashed. "He wants to get rid of me, doesn't he!"

"Of course not!" Dad said. "You don't *have* to move. He just made the offer."

Mrs. Weston thought for a moment. She said, "What about my Bill's chair?"

"I'm sure it would fit in, right next to the window," Dad said.

"What about Kitty?" Mrs. Weston asked nervously.

"Kitty can go with you. We'll take her to the vet first so she'll never be bothered with kittens again," Dad said.

Mrs. Weston leaned forward. "The kittens! What about her kittens?"

Mom said, "I think it would be a good idea to find homes for them. Kiri could put up a sign at the convenience store to let people know about them."

"Maybe we could keep one for ourselves!" Kirandip said hopefully.

Dad acted as if he were about to protest, but Mom gave him a look and he thought better of it. "Well…"

"I could ask around at school to see if anybody wants one!" Kirandip said.

"Good idea!" Mom said.

Mrs. Weston said, "If I moved, would you still come visit me?"

"Every day – just like always," Kirandip said. She meant it.

Mrs. Weston had been her first friend in her new home, and if it hadn't been for her, and the cat, and the kittens...

For the moment, however, Kirandip was busy deciding what her signs for the store and for school would say.

FREE KITTENS!
2 spunky orange tigers
3 cuddly tortoiseshells
2 gray and brown clowns
555-3273

Kirandip's heart sang. If that didn't break the ice, nothing would.

About the Author

I remember when I was little, telling a story I'd made up about crocodiles at a party. I knew then that I wanted to be a writer. I used to write stories at school and pass them around class.
I was always in trouble for it. If I were stuck on a desert island, I wouldn't care as long as I had plenty of pencils and paper.

The idea for this story came when a friend rescued a cat that was having kittens. I thought, what if the kittens had kittens, and then they had kittens...?

Irene Yates